IMAGES
of America

FORT MEADE

PEACEKEEPER OF THE BLACK HILLS

WORLD WAR I RECRUITING POSTER. This US Army recruiting poster by Horst Schreck reads, "The horse is man's noblest companion. Join the cavalry and have a courageous friend." (Courtesy of the Library of Congress, LC-USZC4-1350.)

ON THE COVER: PASS IN REVIEW. In this photograph from 1913 the 12th Cavalry is preparing to pass in review. Pass in review is a long-standing military tradition that began as a way for a newly appointed commander to inspect his troops. Visiting officers or guest speakers may be invited to inspect the troops as well. (Courtesy of Old Fort Meade Museum.)

IMAGES
of America

Fort Meade
Peacekeeper of the Black Hills

Roberta Sago and Lee Stroschine

ARCADIA
PUBLISHING

ISBN 978-1-4671-2801-8

Published by Arcadia Publishing
Charleston, South Carolina

Printed in the United States of America

Library of Congress Control Number: 2017946537

For all general information, please contact Arcadia Publishing:
Telephone 843-853-2070
Fax 843-853-0044
E-mail sales@arcadiapublishing.com
For customer service and orders:
Toll-Free 1-888-313-2665

Visit us on the Internet at www.arcadiapublishing.com

Dedicated to all the soldiers that served, the families that lived, and the veterans receiving medical care at Fort Meade

Contents

ACKNOWLEDGMENTS

We would like to thank the staff and the board of directors of the Old Fort Meade Museum (www.fortmeademuseum.org) for their support and encouragement of this project. All images not attributed to another source come from the museum. We also owe a debt of gratitude to Bob Lee (1920–2005) for all his work on the history of Fort Meade. He was our inspiration and greatest resource for this book.

INTRODUCTION

Gold, the amazing metal, brought men to the Black Hills. The first known incident of prospectors in the Black Hills was in 1833. Ezra Kind and a group came to the hills in search of gold. A sandstone slab was discovered near Spearfish in 1887 with carvings on it by Ezra Kind. On one side of the carving, Kind wrote, "Came to these hills in 1833 seven of us, De Lacompt, Ezra Kind, G. W. Wood, T. Brown, R. Kent, Wm. King, Indian Crow all dead but me Ezra Kind, Killed by Ind beyond high hill got our gold June 1834." On the other side is an inscription that reads, "Got all the gold we could carry our ponies all got by the Indians I have lost my gun and nothing to eat and Indians hunting me." What happened to Ezra Kind and the gold is unknown.

There was no other mention of gold in the Black Hills until 1874. In that year, Lt. Col. George Custer led the 7th Cavalry on an expedition from Fort Abraham Lincoln, in present-day North Dakota, to the Black Hills. The expedition was to explore the Black Hills and find a suitable location for a military post. With the expedition were several scientists as well as two mining experts, five newspaper correspondents, a photographer, and a number of civilians. While camped in the area near the present-day city of Custer, the civilians that had accompanied the expedition discovered gold along French Creek. The word was sent east that gold was found, and a gold rush began.

The first party of the rush came in December 1874 under the leadership of John Gordon. However, in the spring of 1875, the US Cavalry escorted the party out of the area because they were in violation of the Fort Laramie Treaty of 1868. The treaty had guaranteed the Lakota ownership of the Black Hills and other lands in South Dakota, Wyoming, and Montana as the Great Sioux Reservation. The US government decided in November 1875 that the Army should stop removing the trespassers from the Great Sioux Reservation. The government also ordered that all the Lakota return to the reservation by January 1, 1876, or face military action. The Lakota did not return due to the short notice and the winter weather. This order eventually led to Custer's defeat at the Battle of Little Bighorn in June 1876.

By the summer of 1876, thousands of miners and settlers were in the area of Deadwood. Deadwood had become the center of the Black Hills gold rush. In July 1876, the citizens of Deadwood sent a petition to the US government requesting a permanent military post in the Black Hills. Gen. Phillip Sheridan, commander of the Division of the Missouri, responded that any action would have to wait new negotiations with the Lakota to give up the Black Hills. That new agreement with the Lakota was ratified on February 22, 1877. However, this agreement did not end Lakota attacks on the miners and settlers in the Black Hills. Appeals again were made by the settlers and also by the territorial government for a military post. A bill was introduced in Congress in April 1878 to establish a post in the Black Hills.

This new post was to be situated near the convergence of the Bismarck, Pierre, and Sidney roads. It was to have a year-round water supply and an abundance of trees. The 7th Cavalry was sent to establish the post. The 7th Cavalry was under the command of Col. Samuel Sturgis, whose son James had been killed with Custer at the Battle of Little Bighorn. In the 7th Cavalry were also a number of survivors of that battle, including Maj. Marcus Reno and Capt. Frederick Benteen. The first camp location, known as Camp Sturgis and named for Lt. James Sturgis, was located near Bear Butte. It was determined that this location did not fit the needs, most importantly water and trees, so a new location was found. This new location was initially named Camp Ruhlen. Camp Ruhlen was established as a construction camp in August 1878. This camp was renamed on December 31, 1878, as Fort Meade in honor of Civil War general George Meade.

The 7th Cavalry remained at Fort Meade until 1888. It was the first of several military units that were stationed at Fort Meade during the years of its existence. It was during the 7th Cavalry's assignment to Fort Meade that Major Reno was court martialed by Colonel Sturgis for conduct unbecoming an officer and discharged from the Army.

The 7th Cavalry was joined by the 25th Infantry, the buffalo soldiers, in August 1880. The 25th Infantry remained at Fort Meade until May 1888. The 8th Cavalry was then stationed at Fort Meade from 1888 until 1898. The 8th Cavalry was commanded by Col. Caleb Carlton. Colonel Carlton was the officer who began the custom of playing "The Star-Spangled Banner" at military ceremonies. The 8th Cavalry was replaced in 1898 by the 1st Cavalry. The 1st Cavalry remained only until 1901.

It was during the residency of the 13th Cavalry that the wooden structures at Fort Meade were replaced by stone and brick structures. This construction would be completed by 1911.

The 4th Cavalry was the longest serving unit at Fort Meade. They arrived in 1907 and remained until 1911. After the 4th Cavalry left, Fort Meade housed only small units of troops, except for a brief period when the 12th Cavalry was stationed prior to World War I. During the early 1920s, Fort Meade at times only had a small caretaker force stationed there. The 4th Cavalry returned in 1924 and was the last remaining cavalry unit at Fort Meade in 1944.

During the 4th Cavalry's second time at Fort Meade, they were part of the *Explorer* balloon launches conducted by the US Army Air Corps and the National Geographic Society. The *Explorer* balloon reached a then record height of 72,395 feet. Also during the time of the 4th Cavalry at Fort Meade, a Civilian Conservation Corps (CCC) camp, Camp Fechner, was established. Camp Fechner was the headquarters camp for the CCC program in South Dakota.

World War II saw the end of a cavalry presence with the departure of the 4th Cavalry. The site of Camp Fechner was reused and opened as a prisoner of war (POW) camp for German prisoners. These POWs were used to build a Veterans Administration hospital on the grounds of Fort Meade. The hospital was opened in 1945 and is still in use. Fort Meade is also currently the Regional Training Institute for the South Dakota National Guard.

One

Establishing the Fort and the 7th Cavalry 1878–1888

Mata Paha–Bear Butte. The Lakota Sioux call this mountain Mata Paha or Bear Mountain. They believe that it is the most powerful land, a sacred place where the creator has chosen to communicate with the people through vision quests and prayer. In addition to the Lakota Sioux, many other tribes, including the Cheyenne and the Omaha, consider this a sacred place. Located on the east side of the Black Hills, Bear Butte is a striking and awe-inspiring landmark. This cone of igneous rock was formed by volcanic forces but never erupted. It rises 1,400 feet out of the surrounding plains, peaking at 4,422 feet above sea level. As a readily identifiable feature, it was a good rendezvous site. It is also near the confluence of several wagon routes, making locating Fort Meade particularly advantageous. (Courtesy of the Leland D. Case Library, Black Hills State University.)

George Armstrong Custer. George Armstrong Custer was born on December 5, 1839. He was raised in Michigan and Ohio. He attended West Point, graduating last in his class in 1861. He was part of several successful battles during the Civil War where he served in the Union army. He was promoted to lieutenant colonel of the newly formed 7th Cavalry Regiment in July 1866. The 7th Cavalry was stationed at Fort Riley, Kansas, from where they would fight the Indian Wars. In 1874, Custer led an expedition into the Black Hills to find a suitable location for a fort. (Courtesy of the Library of Congress, LC-DIG-ppmsca-39810.)

Custer's Expedition of 1874. George Custer's 1874 expedition to the Black Hills camped approximately three miles from Fort Meade. This photograph from the early 1970s shows Richard B. Williams and Freeman Steele Sr. by the marker that identified the location of Custer's encampment. Williams was the first president of the Old Fort Meade Museum and Historic Research Association and was a guiding force behind the preservation of the buildings at Fort Meade.

Custer's Safe. According to the information on the back of this image, this old, 600-pound safe once belonged to the US Army's famed 7th Cavalry, which was transferred to the newly established Fort Meade from Fort Abraham Lincoln, near Bismarck in the Dakota Territory, in 1878. This safe, no doubt, held all the "valuables" of the 7th Cavalry during its tenure here from 1878 until 1888, when it was then transferred to Fort Riley, Kansas. Cavalry units traditionally traveled light to enhance their mobility, so when the move to Fort Riley was made, one of the items left behind was this safe. A Sturgis pioneer lumberman named William Grams picked up the safe from Fort Meade in 1907 as surplus property while building structures at the fort. Grams shoved the safe under the stairs at his sawmill, and there it reposed until 1971. His descendants donated it to the museum.

Safe at Sawmill. This image shows the safe under the stairs at William Gram's sawmill on Lazelle Street in Sturgis, South Dakota.

Camp Jack Sturgis. The area around Bear Butte was deemed a desirable place for a fort because it had ample resources, including a constant water supply, wood for fuel, and ample grass to make hay to feed the horses. It was also near the convergence of the Bismarck, Pierre, and Sidney roads leading into the Black Hills. In July 1878, Companies A, C, D, E, G, I, K, and M of the 7th Cavalry, under the leadership of Col. Samuel Sturgis, made a 12-day march from Fort Lincoln to establish the "Camp at Bear Butte." (Courtesy of South Dakota State Archives.)

Jack Sturgis. The camp at Bear Butte was later named for J.G. Sturgis. Lt. James G. Sturgis was the oldest son of Col. Samuel Sturgis. James graduated from the US Military Academy in 1875 and was appointed second lieutenant with the 7th Cavalry under the command of his father. James was killed at the Battle of Little Bighorn on June 25, 1876, and his body was never recovered. (Courtesy of the Bob Lee Papers, Leland D. Case Library, Black Hills State University.)

Lt. George Ruhlen. Lt. George Ruhlen was born in Germany in 1847 and immigrated to America with his parents in 1852. Ruhlen graduated from the US Military Academy in 1872 and was commissioned second lieutenant with the 17th Infantry. In 1878, Ruhlen was the regimental quartermaster of the 17th Infantry and was assigned to oversee the construction of a new fort at the edge of the Black Hills. The new post was initially named Camp Ruhlen. It was officially designated Fort Meade on December 31, 1878. Ruhlen also oversaw the construction of the new Fort Bliss in Texas from 1891 to 1894 and the rebuilding of Fort Riley in Kansas from 1896 to 1898. Ruhlen served as quartermaster in different commands until his retirement as colonel in 1911. Colonel Ruhlen was recalled to duty in 1916 and again served as quartermaster until 1918. Ruhlen died in 1933.

MAJ. HENRY M. LAZELLE. Maj. Henry M. Lazelle graduated from the US Military Academy at West Point in 1855. He was commissioned as a second lieutenant with the 8th Infantry. Lazelle served throughout the Civil War. He was promoted to major of the 1st Infantry in 1874. In 1878, Lazelle was ordered to oversee the construction of a new post in the Black Hills. This post was called Camp Ruhlen at first; the name was changed in December 1878 to Fort Meade. Lazelle was the first post commander of Fort Meade and remained at Fort Meade until May 1879, when he was appointed commandant of the Corps of Cadets at the US Military Academy. Lazelle was appointed lieutenant colonel of the 23rd Infantry in 1881. He served until his retirement in 1894. (Courtesy of James Carson.)

MAJ. GEN. GEORGE MEADE. Fort Meade was named after Gen. George Meade, who died in 1872. Meade graduated from the US Military Academy in 1835 and was commissioned as second lieutenant in the 3rd Artillery. Meade served during the war with Mexico, from 1846 to 1847. He then served as an engineer until the start of the Civil War. Meade was promoted to brigadier general of volunteers in 1861 and rose to the rank of major general in the US Army in 1864. Meade was the commander of the Army of the Potomac at the Battle of Gettysburg in 1863. Meade continued to command until his death in 1872. (Courtesy of the Library of Congress, LC-DIG-ppmsca-40717.)

COMMISSARY SERGEANT'S QUARTERS. The commissary sergeant was the second-highest ranking enlisted man behind the sergeant major. He was responsible for all aspects of caring for the food supplies. He managed the storehouse to ensure that food did not spoil before it was used. He was also responsible for dispersing the prescribed quantities to the troops.

THE COMMISSARY STOREHOUSE. Dry goods and related supplies were stored in the commissary storehouse. This was overseen by the commissary sergeant, who, in addition to managing the supplies, was responsible for their security. This was the first building constructed at Fort Meade in 1878 and the only original structure standing today.

Root House. Perishable foodstuffs required more care in storage; vegetables were kept in the root house. It was connected to the commissary storehouse and measured 100 by 26 feet and nine feet deep. The root house was later used as a civilian defense fallout shelter during the 1950s. (Courtesy of the South Dakota State Archives.)

The Bakery. Under the responsibly of the mess sergeant, the bakery provided fresh bread to the commissary for distribution. The bakery produced up to 700 18-ounce loaves a day.

Sawmill. Local timber and locally quarried stone were used to build the fort. A sawmill was required to transform the timber into usable lumber. The Fort Meade sawmill was located beyond the current west entrance to the fort. On December 1, 1880, the quartermaster's office hired Calvin Duke as the engineer and surveyor to run the sawmill. This local man was also a partner in the Northwest Hotel in Sturgis. His partner was John Scollard, who also owned the Scollard Hotel. Duke and his wife had four children. Only one daughter grew to adulthood. Their youngest son Jessie died at about one year of age and is buried at the old Fort Meade Cemetery. (Courtesy of the South Dakota State Archives.)

Original Saddlers and Blacksmith Shop. This first shop for saddlers and blacksmiths sat at the west end of the post. Being an Army saddler required a special set of skills. The saddler was responsible for the repair of all harnesses, saddles, and other leather equipment issued to the soldiers. (Courtesy of the South Dakota State Archives.)

Carpenter and Tin Shop. The carpenter was responsible for maintenance of the buildings and making and repairing furniture and any other needed wooden implements. The tinsmith would have made and repaired any items made of tin, such as mess kits, pots, and pans.

Blacksmith and Wheelwright Shop. The blacksmith worked with any item made of iron, including horseshoes, nails, hinges, door latches, and spikes. He was also responsible for maintaining and repairing tools such as axes, shovels, knives, etc. The wheelwright built and maintained the wheels for any vehicle on post.

Reservoir. In 1881, the government appropriated additional funds for the building of Fort Meade. One of the additions made at that time was the reservoir for better managing water resources for the fort.

The Original Stables. Each cavalry company at the fort would have its own stable. This photograph from the 1890s shows the stable for the B Troop of the 8th Cavalry. Each stable held approximately 80 horses and tack (saddles, bridles, etc.). The first stables were completed in 1879 and measured 200 by 30 feet. Like many of the other buildings, they were made of locally cut pine on a foundation of locally mined sandstone.

The Quartermaster Stable. The quartermaster stable was also known by the name mule barn. The quartermaster was responsible for all the supplies needed at the fort. This stable was where the supply wagons and mules or horses used to pull them were kept.

FORT MEADE IN 1888. Visible in the foreground are the officers' quarters, some of which were duplexes, allowing more than one officer and his family to live there. The open area between the buildings is the parade ground. On the other side of the parade ground are the barracks where the enlisted men lived. The headquarters is between the barracks with the flagpole in front of it. Behind the barracks are the stables where the horses were kept. At left, by the trees, is laundress row, where the women, often wives of enlisted men, lived and did the laundry. In the background is Bear Butte.

Officers' Row. Officers with families were housed in single family homes or duplexes. The fort commander resided in the largest house, located in the center of the row and directly across from the headquarters building. The other officers selected the house to live in based on rank. Typically, the lieutenant colonels lived in the houses on either side of the colonel. Pictured here is the original officers housing built between 1878 and 1879.

Bachelor Officers' Quarters. Unmarried officers were housed in the bachelor officers' quarters. They had private rooms and shared a bathroom, a kitchen, and a parlor.

The Barracks. The barracks were where the enlisted men lived. This wood building was the first barracks constructed on the fort. A barracks would usually hold the enlisted men of an entire company—about 80 men. The sergeants would have their own private room while the privates and corporals would share one large common area.

The Barracks Interior. This is the interior of an enlisted barracks. Each trooper had his own bunk. The trunk at the foot of the bunk was for personal items and underclothing. Shoes were lined up under the bunk. Hooks on the wall were for hanging uniforms and accoutrements. There was a shelf for headgear. Rifles were kept on racks in the middle of the room. The corporals and the privates with the most time in service would get the bunks closest to the stove in the middle of the room. (Courtesy of the South Dakota State Archives.)

Interior of Officers' Quarters. Officers lived in nicer quarters than the enlisted men. The higher the rank of the officer, the nicer his quarters became. These two photographs from 1897 show the sitting room in the quarters of the commanding officer, who was Col. Caleb Carlton at that time. The furnishings show the lifestyle that the commander enjoyed. The commanding officer would entertain all the officers in his command with formal social functions and would also host smaller, informal activities with only a few officers. The commanding officer's wife would also entertain the wives of other officers in the same ways. (Courtesy of the South Dakota State Archives.)

Whist Game. Cavalry officers did not socialize with enlisted men. Here is a photograph from June 1897 showing a group of officers playing whist. The officers are in commanding officer Col. Caleb Carlton's quarters. Colonel Carlton is turned facing the camera; the other officers are unidentified. Caleb Carlton graduated from the US Military Academy in 1859 and served during the Civil War. Carlton was appointed colonel of the 8th Cavalry in January 1892. He was promoted to brigadier general just prior to his retirement in 1897. Carlton died in 1923. (Courtesy of the South Dakota State Archives.)

Hospital. In 1879, a single-story hospital was built. It had two wards containing 12 beds each. In 1881, another ward with 12 beds was added. The hospital was further expanded in 1888 when a second story was added. Additional facilities on the ground floor included a kitchen, dining room, stewards' room, dispensary, two offices, a bathroom, and a special ward. The second floor contained one regular ward and one isolation ward, a nurses' room, linen closet, washroom, and a large storage room. In this photograph, the hospital stewards are lined up on the second-story porch.

New Hospital. The *Annual Report of the Secretary of War for the year 1895* indicates that on March 2, the government approved funds in the amount of $25,000 for a new hospital at Fort Meade. The prices contracted for the project included $16,611 for "construction proper," $5,200 for hot water heating, and $1,302 for plumbing and gas piping. At the same time, there was $75.94 appropriated for hospital stewards' quarters. The new hospital was opened toward the end of 1895.

Hospital Stewards' Quarters. Each post was assigned one physician and one hospital steward. After the Civil War, procedures were implemented to make sure that only the most qualified of enlisted men earned the position of hospital steward. They were required to take a test that proved they could write and had proficiency in math and chemistry. This home was later moved to Williams Street in Sturgis.

Nurses Training. Under the supervision of hospital steward Dr. William Munch, nurses are shown here training in Wyoming in 1890. Munch and his family resided in the house next to the hospital where his daughter Marie Munch Laugerman, a future resident of Rapid City, was born. Dr. Munch later became a well-known physician in Linton, North Dakota, where he died in his home in 1911.

Guard Mount of 8th Cavalry. These troopers of the 8th Cavalry are in formation for guard mount. Guard mount was done every morning after roll call. The designated soldiers were assigned to guard duty for 24 hours. Soldiers were selected from different companies, so no one company was undermanned. The soldiers were required to remain in their uniforms with equipment ready for their entire duty. The soldiers would spend two hours on sentry duty and then two hours at the guardhouse. While at the guardhouse the soldiers could relax somewhat, but while on sentry duty, the soldier had to remain vigilant because he was the security, police, and fire watch for the fort.

Original Guardhouse. This is the first guardhouse at Fort Meade; it was constructed of wood. The guardhouse served as the location for the guard mount as well as housing prisoners. A portion of the guardhouse held cells for the prisoners. The rest of the guardhouse was the quarters for the soldiers on guard mount duty. There would be a bunk for the soldiers to rest on while not on sentry duty.

Hook and Ladder Company. This is the Fort Meade Hook and Ladder Company in 1891. The hook and ladder company in a fire department was responsible for rescuing people from windows or providing access for firemen and tearing down walls with their long hooked poles. The hook and ladder wagon was pulled to the scene by the firemen.

Wet Hose Company. These troopers of Company B, 7th Cavalry were the winners of a wet hose race at Fort Meade on July 4, 1887. Their names are W. Everson, J. Mullican, M. Hagmuller, W.F. Marlow, T.H. Kud, F. Sheridan, H. Ricney, J.H. Adams, P.E. Conley, E.C. Gilman, C. Rayman, L. Roboson, J.J. Dwyer, A. McCann, and J.H. Burnett. The hose company would bring the hose to a fire and spray the water that was supplied by the fire engine. Wet hose races were competitions between different fire departments. (Courtesy of the South Dakota State Archives.)

Magazine. Ammunition was stored in special building away from the other structures on the fort. This building was known as the magazine. It was constructed to be fireproof. This magazine at Fort Meade was made of brick with a tin cover door to keep any fire from entering the building. The magazine would contain the ammunition for the rifles, pistols, and artillery pieces of the regiment. (Courtesy of the South Dakota State Archives.)

Ordnance Warehouse. The ordnance warehouse was where the weapons used by the soldiers were stored. These weapons would include extra rifles, pistols, and sabers not issued to the soldiers as well as extra leather gear used with the weapons. Also stored in the warehouse were the artillery pieces and associated ammunition caissons. (Courtesy of the South Dakota State Archives.)

Headquarters Building. The headquarters building is the center of the military on the fort. Headquarters was the location of the commanding officer's office, the administration office, and the post office. Headquarters was where the soldiers went to request leave, pick up their pay, and receive punishment for minor offenses. New soldiers and officers were required to report to headquarters on their arrival at a new post. This photograph shows the first headquarters building at Fort Meade. It was replaced with a larger two-story building.

Fort Meade with Bear Butte. Fort Meade, like so many other western forts, was an open post with no stockade to surround it. This image shows the fort buildings from the 1880s. Visible at upper left is "Soap Suds Row" where the laundresses lived and worked. The Fort Meade Military Reserve, which was all the land the Army set aside for the fort, was roughly six miles north to south and two miles east to west. The large size of the reserve was to limit settlement by civilians near the post who could discipline problems for the soldiers. The land of the reserve outside the fort buildings was used for field training exercises, firing ranges, and cavalry jumps.

Col. Samuel Davis Sturgis. Col. Samuel Davis Sturgis serve in the military for 40 years. The fifth child of James and Mary (Brandesbury) Sturgis, of Shippensbury, Pennsylvania, he graduated from the US Military Academy at West Point in 1846. Sturgis first served in the Mexican war as well as in a number of Indian campaigns throughout the 1850s, until the Civil War broke out. After the Civil War, Lieutenant Colonel Sturgis was assigned to the 6th Cavalry in Texas. On July 3, 1868, he was assigned to the Board of Cavalry Tactics. He was promoted to colonel of the 7th Cavalry on May 6, 1878, and joined the regiment in Louisville, Kentucky, for Reconstruction duty. From October 1874 until October 1876, he was assigned commander of the Cavalry Depot in St. Louis, Missouri, and thus missed the fateful Battle of Little Big Horn, which took his oldest son. He rejoined the 7th Cavalry on October 20, 1876. Colonel Sturgis took command of Fort Meade in July 1879 and retired in 1886.

Ella Sturgis. Ella Sturgis, born in 1859, was the third child of Col. Samuel Sturgis. She came with her family to Fort Meade in 1879. Ella received the attention of many of the single officers while at Fort Meade. She later married a prominent banker from Mitchell, South Dakota. Ella died in 1925.

Maj. Marcus Reno. Maj. Marcus Reno graduated from the US Military Academy in 1857. He served as a cavalry officer during the Civil War. He joined the 7th Cavalry in 1871. At the Battle of Little Big Horn, Reno was second-in-command to Lt. Colonel George Custer. Reno and most of those under his command survived the battle. Reno took command of Fort Meade in May 1879 after serving a court martial sentence of two years for making unwanted advances toward the wife of another officer. Reno served as commander until July 1879 when Col. Samuel Sturgis arrived and took over. Reno again faced a court martial, this time by Colonel Sturgis in 1880 for conduct unbecoming an officer; he was accused of drunkenness and window peeping at Colonel Sturgis's daughter Ella. Reno was convicted and dismissed from the service. However, in 1967 a military board of review examined his case and reversed the judgment, changing his discharge to honorable, and ordered his remains to be reinterred at the site of the Battle of Little Bighorn. He died in 1889.

Comanche. The most famous equine to reside at Fort Meade was Comanche, the lone military horse to survive the Battle of Little Big Horn. Comanche, a buckskin, stood 15 hands high. He had a black mane and tail, a white fetlock, white spots on his back, and a small white star on his forehead. Found bloody and emaciated after the battle, he was transported by steamer to Bismarck in the Dakota Territory and then by wagon Fort Lincoln, Nebraska. Comanche recovered from his battle wounds the spring of 1878. On April 10, 1878, Col. Samuel Sturgis, who had lost his son at the Battle of Little Big Horn, issued the command that no one would be permitted to ride Comanche. In the spring of 1879, Comanche came to Fort Meade when the regiment was transferred there. In July 1887, he returned to Fort Riley in Kansas with the Band and Troops C, D, G, and M. He died at approximately 29 years of age on November 6, 1891.

Two

End of the Frontier 1889–1900

Paymaster's Wagon. Important to the soldiers at Fort Meade was their pay. These soldiers are guarding the paymaster on his way to Fort Meade in 1888. Payday for the soldiers had been changed in 1887 from every two months to every month. The paymaster is on the Deadwood road to Fort Meade. Deadwood was the main economic center of the Black Hills in the 1880s. (Courtesy of the Library of Congress, LC-DIG-ppmsc-02608.)

Native American Soldiers. This is a group of Lakota men who were part of Troop L, 3rd Cavalry. Troop L was stationed at Fort Meade from the fall of 1891 until disbanded in 1894. With the troopers is chaplain Edward Vattman, who served many years in the Army. Father Vattman was well liked by the Lakota and learned to speak their language.

Native American Troops. This photograph from late 1891 shows Troop L, 3rd Cavalry. Troop L was made up of Native American men. These men were recruited from the Cheyenne River Reservation in South Dakota and were mostly members of the Miniconjou, Two Kettle, Sans Arc, and Blackfoot groups of the Lakota people. The US Army began recruiting Native Americans early in 1891. Troop L was commanded by 1st Lt. Godfrey H. MacDonald, seated in the first row with a saber. Lieutenant MacDonald was assisted by 1st Sgt. James Chasing Hawk, seated second from the left in the first row.

Buffalo Soldiers. The 25th Infantry Regiment was formed in 1866 after the Civil War. It was one of four segregated units in the Army at that time. The 25th Infantry was stationed at Fort Meade beginning in 1880 and remained until 1888. During that time, there were four companies assigned to Fort Meade—A, D, H, and K. This photograph is of Company H, 25th Infantry in front of the barracks. The segregated Army units were commanded by white officers, as seen by the three officers standing on the steps behind the soldiers.

The 4th Cavalry Regiment. This image from July 17, 1909, shows the 4th Cavalry in formation at Fort Meade. The commanding officer and staff are on the right. In the center are Companies

A, B, C, D, I, K, L, and M with the officer of each company in front and the first sergeant on the right. The band is on the left mounted on white horses.

BEAR BUTTE PASS. Lt. Col. Edwin Vose Sumner Jr., commander of the 8th Cavalry, returned to Fort Meade through Bear Butte Pass from Sturgis, South Dakota. Throughout the Civil War, Sumner served several different units. Sumner was at Fort Meade from 1891 to 1894. He left when he was promoted to colonel in command of the 7th Cavalry.

MANEUVERS NEAR DEVIL'S TOWER, WYOMING. The 6th Cavalry was stationed at Fort Meade from 1890 to 1893 and again from 1903 to 1907. These troops of Company B were part of large-scale maneuvers in Wyoming in the summer of 1906.

National Salute. This image shows soldiers of the 8th Cavalry firing the National Salute on July 4, 1897. The artillery piece is a Model 1857 12-pounder Napoleon towed field gun. The Model 1857 was first used during the American Civil War and remained in use until the early 1900s.

Horses Lying Down. The horse was the most important thing to the cavalry trooper. Without the horse, the trooper would be stranded. Troopers taught their horses to lie down to make them a smaller target from enemy fire. This photograph shows troopers of the 8th Cavalry with their horses lying down. (Courtesy of the Egge Collection, Sturgis Public Library.)

8TH CAVALRY, JULY 1892. Here are the officers of the 8th Cavalry at Fort Meade in July 1892. Col. Caleb Carlton, commanding officer of the 8th Cavalry and Fort Meade, is seated in the middle of the back row. The other senior officers at that time were Lt. Col. Edwin V. Sumner and Maj. Almond B. Wells.

8TH CAVALRY BUGLERS. Buglers were an important part of the cavalry. Bugle calls were used to indicate changes in the routines of the fort. Some of those calls for the cavalry were Boots and Saddles, used to signal the troopers to get their horses and get prepared; Guard Mount to signal the troopers to assemble for guard duty; and Mess Call to signal the troopers that the meal was ready. This photograph from 1894 shows the buglers from the 8th Cavalry by the gazebo at Fort Meade. (Courtesy of the South Dakota State Archives.)

Sharpshooter Target Practice. John A. Miller (center) is firing the first rifle sharpshooter at 800 yards at Fort Meade in 1888. He was a member of Troop C, 8th Cavalry.

Company C, 3rd Infantry on Maneuvers. The 3rd Infantry was stationed at Fort Meade from 1888 to 1891. These soldiers are on maneuvers outside the fort in 1890 with Bear Butte in the background. The soldiers are carrying Springfield Model 1884 rifles, also known as "Trapdoors." (Courtesy of the Library of Congress, LC-DIG-ppmsc-02560.)

8th Cavalry on Dress Parade. Troops from the 8th Cavalry are on dress parade at Fort Meade in 1889. The troops are wearing the regulation 1881 cavalry dress helmet. They are being inspected by a senior officer. The regimental band is visible at left.

3rd Infantry, Company C. The 3rd Infantry was stationed at Fort Meade from 1888 to 1890. The difference between infantry and cavalry was that the infantry walked everywhere while the cavalry rode horses. Also the infantry was armed with the Springfield rifle while the cavalry was armed with the Springfield carbine. This image shows the soldiers of 3rd Infantry, Company C armed with their Springfield rifles. (Courtesy of Library of Congress, LC-DIG-ppmsc-02557.)

Three

Social Life 1878–1920

Officers' Wives. Officers' families followed them from post to post. This photograph from 1902 shows the 13th Cavalry officers' wives on the steps of one of the officer's quarters. These higher-ranking officers' wives were the socialites of the fort and formed a kind of sisterhood based on being isolated on the frontier and sharing their unique situation as a participant in Army life. The women in the photograph are not specifically identified; however, officers' wives of this period include Gertrude McElrath Hayes, wife of Col. Edward Hayes, commander of Fort Meade; Clara Medora Church Thomas, wife of Lt. Col. Earl Thomas; Susan Agnes Murphy Hunt, wife of Maj. Levi P. Hunt; and Alice Davies Rochester Fenton, wife of Capt. Charles W. Fenton.

School and Chapel. At Fort Meade, the chaplain was responsible for the education of the children on the post as well as the spiritual well-being of all the residents of the fort. Sometimes the chaplain would allow the children of civilians working on post to attend school with the military children, although it could be up to the post commander's will. The school building shown in the photograph above was constructed in 1888. It still stands, but like most of the buildings on post, it was later covered with a stone facade. The chapel below was built at approximately the same time. It burned down sometime later.

Library and Reading Room. The library and reading room was a place for intellectual pursuits. The post exchange was also housed in this building.

Sleigh Ride. A good tonic for cabin fever is a sleigh ride on a brisk winter day. Here, Fort Meade families are shown on a sleigh ride outing.

American Legion Parade Float. Fort Meade and the military maintained close ties with the Sturgis community by participating in local events such as parades. This parade float is presumed to be from the Fourth of July. It dates from approximately 1920, as shown by the display of the American Legion emblem. The American Legion was founded on September 9, 1919.

Parade, Main Street, Sturgis. Troops from the 8th Cavalry are on parade at First and Main Streets in Sturgis in the late 1880s. Relations between the citizens of Sturgis and the troops of Fort Meade were cordial. The troops are in campaign dress, which they would wear on field maneuvers.

Parade in Sturgis, South Dakota. A cavalry troop from Fort Meade leads a parade for an unidentified occasion on Main Street in Sturgis, South Dakota, in 1893. Pictured is the corner of Main and First Streets.

FAIRS AND SHOWS. The troops at Fort Meade also participated in community fairs and shows. In 1913, the 19th Infantry and the 12th Cavalry participated in Butte County Fair on September 5 and the first Meade County Fair on October 7 and 8. Earlier that year, they participated in a horse show in Deadwood. On May 23, the *Sturgis Weekly Record* reported, "It will be possible for those who attend the horse show to see some of the best horses in the northwest and Lt. Edwards promises that the posts will send some horses that are fancy performers in jumping and spectacular feats."

HOLIDAY CELEBRATIONS. Holidays on an isolated frontier fort, far from family, could be hard on a soldier. To allay the melancholy and create good cheer and comradery, holidays were celebrated with festive meals. This 1897 photograph shows Troop E of the 8th Cavalry barracks mess hall decorated for Christmas dinner.

GYMNASIUM. Athletic pursuits kept the troops fit and busy in their downtime. With the cold South Dakota winters, a facility for indoor activities was needed. The gymnasium, located next to the bachelor officers' quarters, fit the bill. Boxing was the main activity that took place here. It was later used for many purposes, including a post exchange and tailor's shop, officers' club and bar, a post office, a library, and a bowling alley. From the 1940s until about 2000, it was used at the chapel.

Basketball Team, 6th Cavalry. Sports were one of the activities that kept the soldiers occupied in their free time. Providing organized activities could reduce discipline problems brought about by boredom. This photograph shows the basketball team of 6th Cavalry, Troop A in 1906.

Baseball Team, 6th Cavalry. This photograph shows the baseball team of 6th Cavalry, Troop A in 1906. The players are in regular baseball uniforms in contrast to the officer in military uniform seated at left. The officer is Capt. Abraham G. Lott. Captain Lott was an avid baseball player in his youth as well as while at the US Military Academy. Lott graduated from there in 1896 and served as a brigadier general until his retirement in 1935. General Lott died in 1945.

FISHING. The Black Hills offer many types of outdoor activities. These soldiers are finding relaxation while fishing, presumably in Bear Butte Creek, as it is adjacent to the post. Originally, the only fish in Black Hills streams were a type of sucker fish. In 1896, a National Fish Hatchery, also called the Spearfish Station, was founded in Spearfish, South Dakota. They raised and stocked the regional streams and lakes with rainbow and brown trout. By 1970, these fish varieties were reproducing naturally in the Black Hills streams.

CEMETERY. The post cemetery is located on a hill overlooking the main fort grounds with a spectacular view of Bear Butte. The first burials took place in late summer 1878. Pvt. Albert Niehaven, from the 7th Cavalry, Company C, died at Camp Sturgis in August of that year. He was originally buried near Bear Butte but later reinterred at the new cemetery. There are 200 individuals buried at this cemetery. In addition to soldiers, there are 53 children and 16 wives of soldiers in the cemetery. The majority of the burials took place before 1900. The last to be buried in the old post cemetery was Edward R. Gramith, retired first sergeant of the 4th Cavalry, Troop A. He died October 27, 1943. The cemetery was officially closed when the Black Hills National Cemetery was opened just south of the military reservation in 1948.

JAMES PLUNKETT. James Plunkett was a soldier in the 1st Infantry in 1880 at Fort Meade. This photograph shows James and his son William, age 8. James served in the US Army from 1860 to 1880. He died in 1891 at his home near Fort Meade and was buried at the Fort Meade Cemetery.

ELIZABETH PLUNKETT. Elizabeth Torrence Baldwin Plunkett married and outlived three husbands. All three of her husbands were soldiers in the 1st Infantry. Elizabeth had four children with her first husband, Joseph Torrence, and one with her last husband, James Plunkett. After James left the service in 1880, Elizabeth and James homesteaded east of Fort Meade. Elizabeth died at her home in 1907 and is buried in the Fort Meade Cemetery.

ARMY LAUNDRESSES. During the Civil War and the frontier Indian Wars, the Army enlisted laundresses to serve with the regiments. These women were "carried on the rolls" and received pay and rations like the soldiers. The work was back breaking; one laundress would be responsible for the laundry of up to 25 men. They had to carry water and chop their wood. Wet garments, particularly the wool ones, were very heavy. They had to supply their own equipment and make their own soap. However, they were relatively well compensated. That combined with the fact that there were few women on the frontier made them desirable candidates for marriage, and many did marry soldiers. Or the wife of an enlisted man might be taken on as a laundress. One of the laundresses at Fort Meade was Annie Franklin. She is buried at the old Fort Meade Cemetery; unfortunately, no more is known of her but her name and occupation. By the early 1890s, the Army had stopped enlisting laundresses, and the job fell on the soldiers. (Courtesy of Lee Stroschine.)

Four

Rebuilding the Fort 1900–1911

Fort Meade Overview. This overview of Fort Meade was taken sometime between 1905 and 1908. During this time, the US Army updated fort buildings around the country from wood to stone or brick. The two-story barracks in the center of the photograph were updated with three additions on the left made of stone and the two on the right built of brick. The houses in the foreground are officers' quarters.

New Guardhouse/Post Office. At the turn of the 20th century, funding was secured for major renovations at Fort Meade. One of the new structures was the guardhouse. William Grams, of Sturgis, was awarded the contract for several of sandstone buildings, including the new guardhouse. In 1901, Grams had installed the 100-foot iron flagpole on post. He also constructed the Meade County Courthouse in Sturgis. When Fort Meade transitioned to a veterans hospital, the guardhouse became the post office. (Below, courtesy of the Leland D. Case Library, Black Hills State University.)

Preparing for Guard Mount. This photograph from 1913 shows the 13th Cavalry preparing for guard mount. This image shows the changes in the buildings that occurred in the period around 1905. The new guardhouse is seen in the left background. The troopers are armed with M1903 Springfield rifles.

Riding Arena. Bitter South Dakota winters made it necessary to have an indoor space for the soldiers to keep up their riding skills. In 1929, this brick riding arena was built. At the time, it was the largest clear span building of its type in the US Army. During World War II, it was used as a shop to repair tanks and gliders. When the Veterans Administration took over Fort Meade for a hospital, the arena was converted into a gymnasium. (Courtesy of the Leland D. Case Library, Black Hills State University.)

ESTABLISHING THE 13TH CAVALRY. Due the Spanish-American War, soldiers were transferred out of Fort Meade, resulting in a reduction in the number of the cavalry troops. To replenish the garrison, in 1901 the 13th Cavalry Regiment was organized at Fort Meade. It was the first regiment formed there and not assigned to the post after serving elsewhere. The four unidentified cavalry men were members of the 13th Cavalry Regiment; they are outfitted for a special occasion in their undress uniforms as indicated by the gloves and sabers. The undress uniform is used for balls, weddings, and such. The full-dress uniform is used for more formal and ceremonial events. It is distinguished by a more elaborate coat and hat.

19th Infantry. In addition to the cavalry, there were some infantry companies stationed at Fort Meade. The above photograph from 1912 shows Company M of the 19th Infantry. Companies I, K, L, and M were stationed at Fort Meade from June 1912 to February 1913. These soldiers are preparing a meal during field maneuvers. The photograph below, also from 1912, shows the supply wagon on maneuvers near Bear Butte.

Drills. The photograph above shows the 19th Infantry soldiers in shelter tent drills on the Fort Meade parade grounds in 1912. Tents buttoned along the center peak. They accommodated two men, each of which would carry half the tent, one tent pole, and half the tent stakes. Below, the soldiers are marching in formation on the parade grounds.

Decoration Day, 1907. A mounted band troop and four other troops are marching in formation from Sturgis to Fort Meade on Decoration Day, May 30, 1907. Gen. John A. Logan, commander and chief of the Grand Army of the Republic declared Decoration Day as May 30 in 1868. It was established to commemorate those who died in the Civil War by decorating the graves of fallen soldiers with flowers. It became commonly known as Memorial Day after World War II and became an official US holiday celebrating all fallen soldiers in 1967.

Pass in Review, 1913. The 12th Cavalry is preparing to pass in review. The troops are dismounted, meaning that they were not on their horses. Pass in review is a long-standing military tradition that began as a way for a newly appointed commander to inspect his troops. Visiting officers or guest speakers may be invited to inspect the troops as well.

Pass in Review, 1912. Here, the 3rd Squadron of the 12th Cavalry is ready for pass in review and muster. The troops are mounted on their horses with their sabers drawn. Having sabers drawn was the way a cavalry showed respect to the visiting guest who was reviewing them.

Cavalrymen. Typical young cavalrymen Frank Dellitt and Jack Scullen are shown in this studio portrait, which was printed as a postcard and was likely sent to family at home.

Lt. Matt Combes Bristol. Not all officers started their military careers at West Point. Officers commissioned from the enlisted ranks were known as mustangs. One such man was Lt. Matt Combes Bristol. He enlisted as a private in the 7th Cavalry in 1898. Bristol rose through the ranks to become a second lieutenant of the newly formed 13th Cavalry in 1901. This photograph from 1906 shows Bristol as a first lieutenant of the 6th Cavalry. After serving in the 6th Calvary at Fort Meade, Bristol was appointed the aide-de-camp to Brig. Gen. Joseph Duncan, commander of the Department of Texas. During World War I, he served as a major in the Signal Corps, becoming a lieutenant colonel in the Finance Department after the war. He retired as a colonel. Bristol was born February 3, 1872, in Wiltshire, England, and passed away February 26, 1968, at Fort Sam Houston in San Antonio, Texas.

Quartermaster's Office. The quartermaster was responsible for the timely and efficient flow of supplies. He made sure there were wagons to transport supplies to the fort. He was also in charge of making sure there were tables, chairs, bunks, and cooking and heating stoves—all the supplies needed for the Army to function. In this undated photograph, Howard Donaldson (left), a quartermaster's sergeant who enlisted January 28, 1908, and an unidentified man (right) are in the quartermaster's office.

13th Cavalry Drills. These photographs from 1902 show Troops I, K, L, and M of the 13th Cavalry. Above, troops are shown in formation on the field at Fort Meade. This formation was used for roll call or preparation for drill. Below, they are in field encampment training, as indicated by the tents in the background.

LOOKING ACROSS THE FIELD AT THE OFFICERS' QUARTERS. This view, facing south across the parade grounds, shows the officers' quarters and the band rotunda in 1913. Officers' quarters could be either single-family houses or duplexes.

BEAR BUTTE PASS. Here is an overview of the fort after the rebuilding in 1905. This photograph shows all nine cavalry stables at right. The gap in the center of the photograph is Bear Butte Pass, between Fort Meade and the city of Sturgis. Bear Butte Creek runs through the pass and behind the stables as indicated by the tree line at the base of the hills.

Barracks. In contrast to the officers, the enlisted men lived in barracks. One troop would be housed in a barracks building. Each barracks consisted of four large open rooms, two on each floor, where the corporals and privates lived. Sergeants had rooms apart from the enlisted men. The first sergeant had a private room, and the lower-ranking sergeants shared rooms.

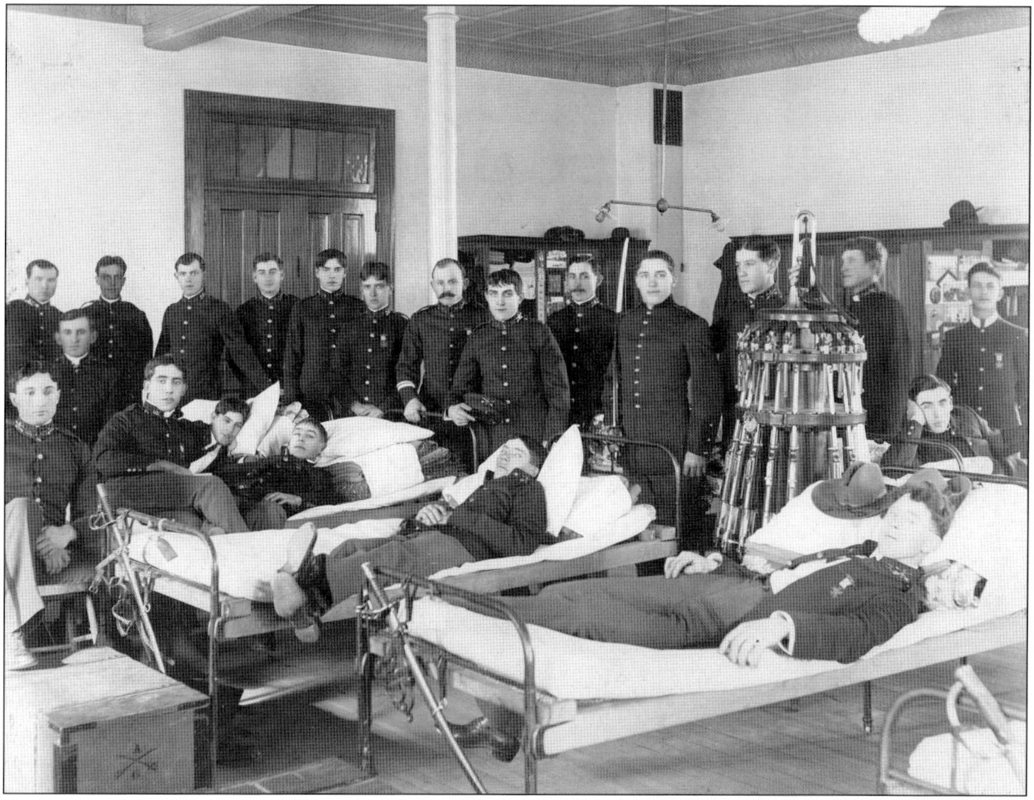

Barracks Interior. This photograph from the early 1900s shows the interior of the enlisted men's barracks of Company A, 6th Cavalry. These were new barracks built during the updating of the fort in the early 1900s. The soldiers' uniforms are from the pre-1903 change made to uniforms. However, the old stock of uniforms was issued until the supply ran out. The weapons rack in the right of the photograph holds M1986 carbines, known as .30-40 Krag. (Courtesy of the South Dakota State Archives.)

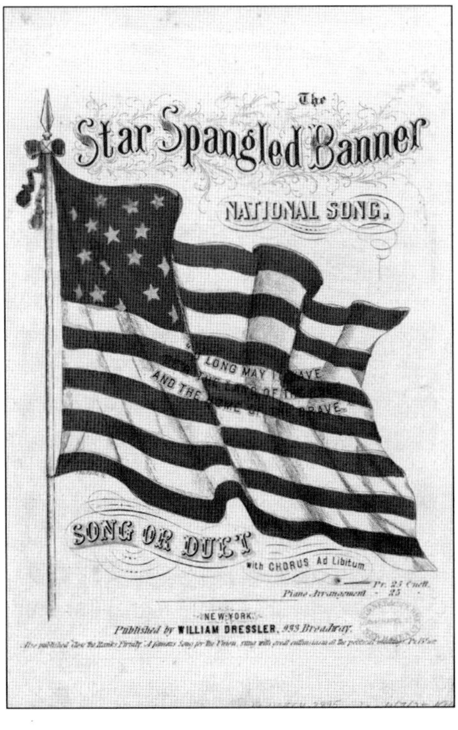

To the Standard. Here, H troop and the band of the 8th Cavalry are lined up in parade formation wearing dress uniforms. The regimental flag can be seen flying next to the American flag. "To the standard" was the ceremonial music that was performed during the parade. H Troop was at Fort Meade from November 1894 through October 1898.

"Star Spangled Banner." Col. Caleb H. Carlton, commander of the 8th Calvary, was the post commander at Fort Meade from February 16 until December 12, 1895. At that time, the United States did not have a national anthem; Carlton felt that one should be selected. In 1892, Colonel Carlton chose the "Star Spangled Banner" to be played at retreat. He chose it for its majesty and the depth of emotion in the events commemorated in it. Colonel Carlton also initiated the tradition of standing and removing one's hat while the song was played. It was not until March 3, 1930, that Congress passed the bill making the "Star Spangled Banner" the national anthem. (Courtesy of the Library of Congress, LC-DIG-ppmsca-31279.)

Ute at Fort Meade. Nearly 20 years after the last battles of the Indian Wars, one last confrontation took place. The White River band of the Ute was particularly disenchanted with reservation life and began fleeing the Unitah Valley of Utah in small groups. In August 1906, the people gathered under Red Cap and Chief and traveled northeast through Colorado and Wyoming. In October, troops from several western forts, including Fort Meade, were sent to intercept the Ute and persuade them to return to the reservation. Upon their refusal to do so, they were escorted to Fort Meade by the 6th Cavalry, under the command of Col. Alexander Rodgers. In November 1906, all arrived at Fort Meade. A camp was set up for the Ute on the southwest side of the military reservation near the site of the old Fort Meade Cemetery.

Ute Portrait. According to Alvin M. Josephy Jr. in his book *Black Hills White Sky*, many of the Ute were put to work on the railroad lines or building fences in Rapid City. This photograph of an unidentified Ute man was taken by well-known Rapid City photographer William J. Collins. (Courtesy of the Leland D. Case Library, Black Hills State University.)

Semi-Abandonment. In 1911, Gen. Leonard Wood proposed a plan to reorganize the Army departments and eliminate small and isolated posts, which included Fort Meade. From 1913 to 1924, Fort Meade was in a period of semi-abandonment. During that time, much discussion took place between local, state, and federal governments regarding whether an Army presence should be maintained at the fort. Finally, thanks to the work of William Williamson, Congressional representative from the 3rd District, military presence was reinstated in 1924. This image of the barns shows the desolation on the post during that time.

Five

PARATUS ET FIDELIS (4TH CAVALRY) 1924–1943

THE 4TH CAVALRY. The 4th Cavalry has the distinction of being the longest serving regiment at Fort Meade. The 4th Cavalry was organized under the act of March 3, 1855. The regiment first came to the Black Hills in 1907. Companies D and F were the first assigned to Fort Meade in March of that year, and by November, the rest of the regiment arrived. They remained until 1911. The 4th Cavalry returned to Fort Meade in 1924 and remained until the beginning of World War II. In this photograph, the 4th Cavalry is on a march near Hot Springs, South Dakota.

HORSE SHOWS. Fort Meade was the location of a number of horse shows and competitions during the 1930s. Here is 1st Lt. John G. Minniece, from the Fort Robinson Remount Depot in Nebraska, competing in the Open Hunter Class at a horse show at the John A. Barry Show Ring in 1937.

HUMAN HURDLE. Members of F Troop show their skills at the Black Hills Round-up in Belle Fourche, South Dakota, in 1931. As noted on the back, "Peewee on horse, Carlson on left."

Goodrich Trophy, 1934. Pictured is A Troop, 4th Cavalry, the winner of the Goodrich Trophy in 1934 and 1935. The Goodrich Trophy was the award for "Cavalry Leadership Test for Small Units." Established in 1924, it tested the leadership of small cavalry units in the US Army. The troop was commanded by 1st. Lt. Carroll H. Prunty.

John A. Barry Trophy. Here is Col. Stanley Koch, commander of the 4th Cavalry, presenting the John A. Barry Trophy to Capt. Louis B. Rapp and 1st Sgt. Bill Williams in 1937. The trophy is named after Col. John A. Barry, commander of the 4th Cavalry, who died in January 1936. Colonel Barry was a two-time Olympic equestrian.

Musical Drills. A musical drill is pictured here at John A. Barry Stadium in 1938. Troopers would show off their ability and that of their horses by performing military drills set to music. This photograph shows Troop E, 2nd Squadron, 4th Cavalry, known as the Bay Horse Troop. The troop commander was Capt. William S. Biddle III, assisted by 1st Sgt. Bill Williams. Captain Biddle graduated from West Point and was commissioned a second lieutenant of cavalry in 1923. Captain Biddle served in the Army for 37 years, including as commanding officer of the 113th Cavalry in combat in Europe during World War II. Biddle retired as a major general in 1960.

Black Horse Troop. F Troop, 4th Cavalry, called the Black Horse Troop, was well known in the Black Hills for its precision drilling. The name Black Horse Troop was given to F Troop because the entire troop was mounted on black horses. This photograph was taken in 1929.

TRUMPETERS. Musicians were an important part of the military. Trumpeters had been used for centuries to sound signals for the soldiers. In the 1840s, the US Army started developing and using bands in the cavalry regiments. All the cavalry regiments in the American West had a band. As with all cavalry soldiers, these band members of the 4th Cavalry are mounted on their horses, with their instruments.

4TH CAVALRY BAND. Music was an integral part of cavalry life. This was the band of the 4th Cavalry in 1927. The members, as listed on the back, are Smith, Eagle Feather, Jullian, unidentified, Olson, Kills-in-Sight, White Horse, Forry, Dees, Martin, Jones, Zimmer, Perry, Schreiner, W.O. Grlinberger, Owens, Capanella, Bittrich, and Feretti.

Polo. The 4th Cavalry established the first known regimental polo club in the US Army in 1892. The Army Polo Association was established in 1902 with clubs organized on military posts. Polo was widely popular in the era between the world wars, and the US Army participated in international competitions during this time. These soldiers from the 4th Cavalry were part of the polo team at Fort Meade in 1927. Four of them are identified: Lt. Ralph Neal (third from left), Lt. A.E. Forsyth (fourth from left), Lieutenant Strawn (fourth from right), and Lt. John Murtaugh (third from right).

Polo Team, 1926. This is the 1926 Fort Meade polo team. From left to right are Lt. John I Gregg III, Captain Fiske, Captain Wall, Lt. John T. Ward, and Lieutenant Stone, of the 4th Cavalry. Lieutenant Ward died on the Bataan Death March in 1944.

Officers' Fox Hunt. Like enlisted men, officers needed rest and relaxation as well. Here, some officers are preparing for a fox hunt in 1937. 1st Lt. William W. Culp is the MFH (Master of Foxhounds). Lieutenant Culp graduated from the US Military Academy at West Point in 1932 and was commissioned into the cavalry. He served in the Pacific theater during World War II and eventually rose to the rank of colonel.

Polo Pony Scurry Race. The troopers liked to show off their skill and the ability of their horses. This photograph from 1937, taken at a horse show, shows a polo pony scurry race. A scurry race is a series of small jumps that the riders go over, then around a marker, and then back over the jumps.

Army Relief Fund-Raising Party, 1936. The theme for the party (held on the second floor of post headquarters building) was "The Stratosphere Bowl." Pictured in the last row are, from left to right, Captain Vergal, MD; 1st Lt. Charles Bixel, E Troop; Major Barrager, regimental S-3; Capt. William S. Biddle, commanding officer, E Troop; 2nd Lt. Kelso S. Clow, A Troop; 1st Lt. Thomas F. Taylor, Machine Gun Troop; Major Robinson, 4th Cavalry (detached from Civilian Conservation Corps duty); Captain Shaw, regimental adjutant; 1st t. Eric H. Svensson, A Troop; Major Upton, 4th Cavalry; Major Nye, veterinarian; 2nd Lt. John F. Rhoades, E Troop; and 2nd Lt. Edward W. Sawyer, B Troop.

Fort Meade Dramatic Club. The Fort Meade Dramatic Club is pictured in 1938. The performers in this play titled *Shh . . . Not So Loud* are, from left to right, Mrs. Washburn, Mary Ingram, Kathleen Nye, Captain Vecqueray, Lottie Rapp, 2nd Lt. Kimo Dunn, 2nd Lt. Kelso Clow, and 2nd Lt. Bob Quinn.

Hockey Team. The long winters at Fort Meade provided opportunities for outdoor activities. These soldiers of the Headquarters Troop, 4th Cavalry are members of a hockey team during the winter of 1928–1929.

Outdoor Activities. Here, Headquarters Troop, 4th Cavalry is having winter fun at Sylvan Lake in Custer State Park. Skiing, ice hockey, and tobogganing were all part of the activities.

Rest and Relaxation. Soldiers did not spend all their time in military duties. These soldiers of F Troop are enjoying some rest and relaxation. In front is Sgt. Joe Grams with Bud, the dog. The soldiers sitting on the porch of the barracks are, from left to right, Privates Matheny, Jergesen, Gauze, and Barton.

Everett Rambow. Written on the back of this photograph is the following: "Everett Rambow with colt. I taught this colt to give me a kiss and also to shake hands (with front foot)." Everett Rambow was from Kansas and served from 1928 to 1931 as a bugler for Headquarters Company, 4th Cavalry at Fort Meade. He left the service to marry the daughter of a local judge.

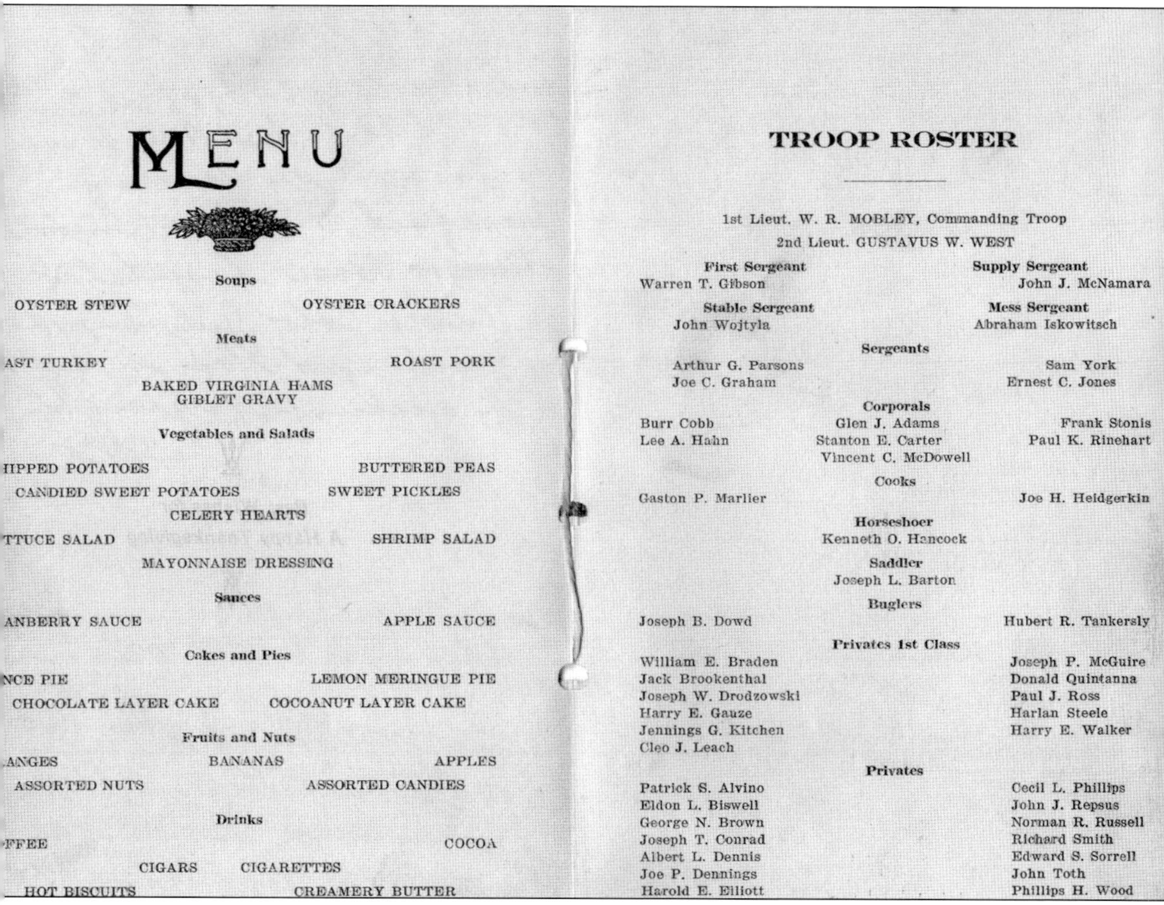

MENU

Soups

OYSTER STEW — OYSTER CRACKERS

Meats

AST TURKEY — ROAST PORK

BAKED VIRGINIA HAMS
GIBLET GRAVY

Vegetables and Salads

IIPPED POTATOES — BUTTERED PEAS

CANDIED SWEET POTATOES — SWEET PICKLES

CELERY HEARTS

TTUCE SALAD — SHRIMP SALAD

MAYONNAISE DRESSING

Sauces

ANBERRY SAUCE — APPLE SAUCE

Cakes and Pies

NCE PIE — LEMON MERINGUE PIE

CHOCOLATE LAYER CAKE — COCOANUT LAYER CAKE

Fruits and Nuts

ANGES — BANANAS — APPLES

ASSORTED NUTS — ASSORTED CANDIES

Drinks

FFEE — COCOA

CIGARS — CIGARETTES

HOT BISCUITS — CREAMERY BUTTER

TROOP ROSTER

1st Lieut. W. R. MOBLEY, Commanding Troop
2nd Lieut. GUSTAVUS W. WEST

First Sergeant
Warren T. Gibson

Supply Sergeant
John J. McNamara

Stable Sergeant
John Wojtyla

Mess Sergeant
Abraham Iskowitsch

Sergeants
Arthur G. Parsons
Joe C. Graham
Sam York
Ernest C. Jones

Corporals
Burr Cobb
Lee A. Hahn
Glen J. Adams
Stanton E. Carter
Vincent C. McDowell
Frank Stonis
Paul K. Rinehart

Cooks
Gaston P. Marlier
Joe H. Heidgerkin

Horseshoer
Kenneth O. Hancock

Saddler
Joseph L. Barton

Buglers
Joseph B. Dowd
Hubert R. Tankersly

Privates 1st Class
William E. Braden
Jack Brookenthal
Joseph W. Drodzowski
Harry E. Gauze
Jennings G. Kitchen
Cleo J. Leach
Joseph P. McGuire
Donald Quintanna
Paul J. Ross
Harlan Steele
Harry E. Walker

Privates
Patrick S. Alvino
Eldon L. Biswell
George N. Brown
Joseph T. Conrad
Albert L. Dennis
Joe P. Dennings
Harold E. Elliott
Cecil L. Phillips
John J. Repsus
Norman R. Russell
Richard Smith
Edward S. Sorrell
John Toth
Phillips H. Wood

THANKSGIVING MENU. Bountiful holiday meals broke up the routine and helped build fellowship among the troops. This menu for a Thanksgiving dinner not only lists the food served but also the soldiers present at the meal.

FIELD INSPECTION. Inspection is one thing that all soldiers have to deal with. This photograph shows a proper field inspection from 1941. This field kit consisted of the clothing worn on the person and the following arms and equipment: saddle; bridle; halter and lead rope; saddle blanket; saddle bags; feed bag for the horse; curry comb; horse brush; lariat; ration bag; mess kit, which included one fork, one knife, and one spoon; first aid kit; cup; canteen and cover; gas mask; cartridge belt with holster; cartridges for the rifle and pistol; and spurs with straps. Not pictured but part of the soldier's field kit was the rifle and scabbard, pistol, and saber and scabbard.

Mealtime. Soldiers need to be fed whether at the fort or in the field. These soldiers are being fed at a field kitchen while on field maneuvers. The soldiers are carrying their mess kits and after getting their food would find a comfortable place to sit on the ground.

Exercises in Pole Mountain, Wyoming. In 1938, the 4th Cavalry participated in an Army exercise in Pole Mountain, Wyoming. This was the last long-distance march of the US Cavalry using horses. The march was about 850 miles round-trip from Fort Meade. This image shows one of the camps along that march.

Horse's Tack. Just as soldiers need to be properly clothed, so do horses. The farrier was the trooper who prepared the horseshoes and applied them to the horses. This farrier has his hammer and anvil and a number of horseshoes. Each horse required the shoes to be fit to its individual hoof, and the farrier performed that task.

Caring for the Horses. The most important duty of a cavalry soldier was caring for his horse. The trooper took care of his horse first thing in the morning before he had breakfast, at noon before lunch, and before supper. Only after his horse was cared for could the trooper tend to himself. These troopers are caring for their horses while on field maneuvers.

TRANSPORTING HORSES. Horses were not always ridden everywhere they needed to go. Here, a horse is being loaded into a truck for transport. The unwilling horse is being assisted by troopers.

SEMITRUCKS. By the 1930s, motorized vehicles had become part of the Army. This photograph shows the semitrucks that were used to transport cavalry troops and their horses. Each semitruck and trailer was capable of hauling eight fully equipped troopers and their horses to any point.

JUMPING. Pictured are Pvt. Robert Green, of Troop E, and his horse, Dusalle. Private Green took first place as the recruit jumper at the 1938 fall horse show at Fort Meade.

JUMPING THROUGH FIRE. Animals are afraid of fire by nature. In order to overcome that fear, cavalry horses had to be trained. These troopers are showing this ability by jumping over burning hurdles at one of the many exhibitions that were done at Fort Meade.

4th Cavalry Horses. Horses are what make soldiers cavalry. Horses for the 4th Cavalry were purchased from a variety of sources. These horses are in the corral next to one of the stables at Fort Meade.

Stable Line, Fort Meade, 1939. Even as the cavalry was transitioning to motor vehicles, the horses were still used. This photograph from 1939 shows the stables, which were used to house horses until the departure of the 4th Cavalry in 1943. The 4th Cavalry's departure brought an end to the use of horses at Fort Meade. Some of the stables were torn down during the construction of the Veterans Administration Hospital. The remaining stables are now used for storage.

A 1935 M1 Scout Car. This photograph from 1939 shows the changes that had taken place in the cavalry over the years. The trooper standing here is holding an M1928A1 Thompson submachine gun. The only thing the Thompson submachine gun had in common with the 1873 Springfield Trapdoor rifle used by the first troops at Fort Meade was the caliber of .45. Behind the trooper is a 1935 M1 Scout Car. The markings on the car indicate it is from the Headquarters Troop, 4th Cavalry.

A 1941 M3 Scout Car. This photograph from 1941 shows Bill Knickerbocker in an M3 Scout Car. Knickerbocker wrote on the back: "Scout car with one mounted 30 caliber, water cooled machine gun. This was a target practice on the moving course. Just a 'dry run.' YES, that's me behind the gun! Note the bar or track under my right arm—the guns are on skates & are movable. Note gun on other car—different position."

Field Exercises, 1941. This photograph was taken of the 4th Cavalry on field exercises in 1941. The following was written on the back: "At this time, the regiment had one horse squadron, one mechanized squadron with Headquarters Troop and Service Troop also mechanized. The mechanized squadron had scout cars (pictured) and motorcycles. 1st Lt. Paul Jolley standing in lead scout car."

Machine Gun Troops. A machine gun troop was organized by the Army in 1916. Originally, these machine gun units were separate squadrons. In 1928, these machine gun squadrons were eliminated, and each cavalry regiment created their own machine gun troop. These soldiers, part of Machine Gun Troop, 4th Cavalry, are shown in front of Building 58 in 1932.

Machine Gun Troop, 4th Cavalry, 1941. This photograph from 1941 shows Machine Gun Troop, 4th Cavalry. It was a separate troop whose function was to supply heavy weapons support for the regiment. The troop was issued M2 Browning .50-caliber heavy machine guns. The M2 Browning machine gun weighed 80 pounds without the weight of ammunition, so it was transported by horse and not by infantry soldiers.

M2 Light Tank, 1936. The M2 Light Tank was introduced to the Army in 1936. This tank had a crew of four: commander/gunner in turret left rear, loader in turret right rear, driver in hull left front, and assistant driver in hull right front.

Lieutenant Hibbert. Lieutenant (Dr.) Hibbert is standing in front of the first training tank to reach Fort Meade. The tank is an M2 Light Tank.

QUARTERMASTER CORPS, 4TH CAVALRY. Shown here is the Quartermaster Corps, 4th Cavalry at Fort Meade in July 1941. The quartermaster is Maj. William E. Vecqueray. Major Vecqueray

began his military career in 1917 as a private in the engineers before accepting a commission in 1919. He ended his service after World War II as a lieutenant colonel.

Preparing for Charge. In preparation for going into combat during World War II, the 4th Cavalry went to Fort Robinson, Nebraska, for training. This photograph, taken on April 6, 1942, shows "The Fighting Fourth Cavalry" preparing to charge. The cavalry never used the horse charge during World War II.

M1 Scout Cars. Pictured are M1 Scout Cars from the Headquarters Company, 4th Cavalry. These troops are watching field maneuvers at Fort Meade.

Veterinary Hospital. Prior to World War I, there was no organized veterinary service for the cavalry. The horses were cared for by the soldiers or the farrier. The US Army established US Army Veterinary Corps in 1916. This 1933 photograph shows the veterinary hospital at Fort Meade at upper right. Also visible are three of the stables, two barracks, and the headquarters building.

Last Major Renovations. The last change to the quarters at Fort Meade occurred during the 1930s when they were veneered with stone. The work was done by the WPA (Works Progress Administration) during 1935 and 1936. This aerial view taken in 1934 shows the buildings prior to that work. Most of these stone veneered buildings still exist.

Baseball Champions. Headquarters Troop, 4th Cavalry at Fort Meade was commanded by Capt. Philip Richard Upton (seated at left of the table) and 1st Lt. John H. Stodter (seated at right of the table). They were the baseball champions of the 4th Cavalry in the spring series 1925. Lt. John Hughes Stodter graduated from the US Military Academy at West Point in 1922 and retired as a colonel after serving during World War II.

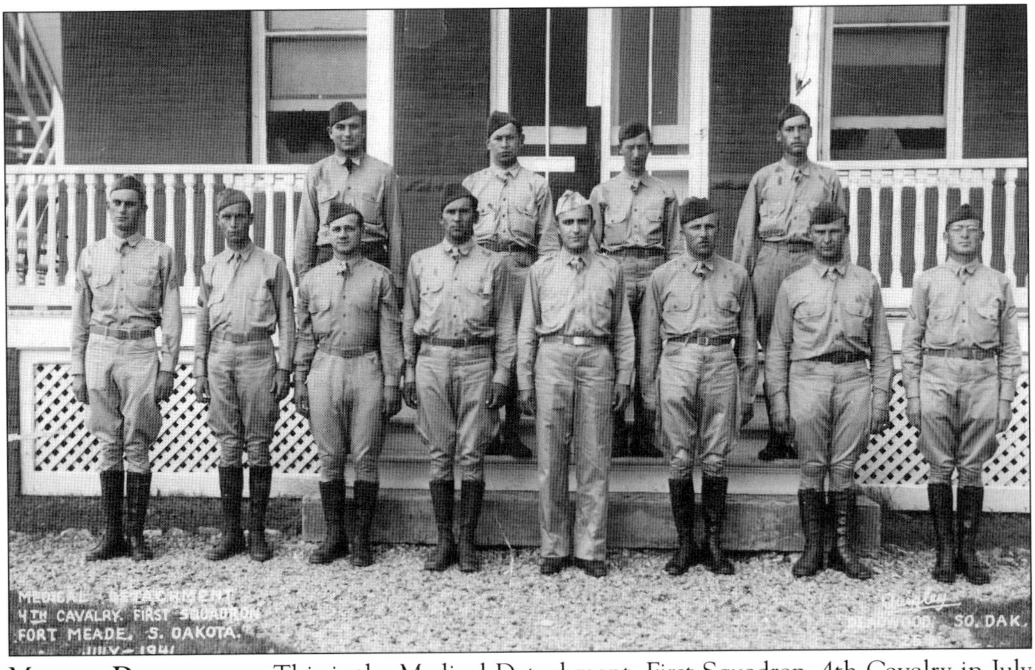

Medical Detachment. This is the Medical Detachment, First Squadron, 4th Cavalry in July 1941 at Fort Meade. The trooper on the right in the second row is Pvt. Tony Alfonso. Private Alfonso wrote the following on the back: "This hear is the Horse outfit and you can see me up there. It was raining that day and we got the drops as you can see on. There I weigh 155 pds now must be around 6 ft don't you think."

COL. STANLEY KOCH. Col. Stanley Koch was the commanding officer of the 4th Cavalry at Fort Meade from 1937 to 1938. Colonel Koch graduated from the US Military Academy in 1904 and had served in the cavalry most of his career. His assignment at Fort Meade was his last duty directly involving troops; he spent the rest of his career in headquarters command.

The Entrance to the Stratobowl Camp. The troopers of the 4th Cavalry referred to this as "Stratocamp." The Stratobowl is located south of Rapid City, South Dakota, and is a natural depression. The Stratobowl was determined by the US Army Air Corps and the National Geographic Society as the best location to launch a balloon to reach the upper atmosphere.

View from the Northwest Rim. This view of the launch site is from the northwest rim 600 feet above the camp. The launch area is the circular area to the left. The tents in the lower right are where the troops were housed. The hydrogen tanks used for *Explorer* are by the trees between the tents and the cars.

STRATOCAMP. The Stratocamp provided all the needs for the troopers assigned there. Drinking water was supplied in large canvas containers. The Stratocamp was used by the troops of the 4th Cavalry during both *Explorer* launches.

TROOP INSPECTION. Troopers of the 4th Cavalry are standing ready for inspection at Stratocamp. Inspections of the troops were held even in the field. The troops are standing with their M1911 Colt pistols ready for inspection.

EXPLORER GONDOLA. This image shows the *Explorer* gondola prior to launch. The gondola was built by the Dow Chemical Company, of Michigan, and was eight feet, four inches in diameter. The crew for *Explorer* was Capt. Albert Stevens, scientific observer; Maj. William Kepner, pilot; and Capt. Orville Anderson.

LAUNCH, JULY 28, 1934. The launch of *Explorer* took place on July 28, 1934. The balloon was 2 1/3 acres in size and held three million cubic feet of hydrogen gas. *Explorer* experienced holes in the balloon, began losing gas, and started an uncontrolled fall. There was also an explosion of the hydrogen gas. The crew was able to bail out and survived uninjured. *Explorer* reached an altitude of 60,613 feet, which was short of the world record at that time.

Hydrogen Tanks. Hydrogen gas was used to inflate the balloon; hydrogen gas had been used in balloons for years. Here are some of the hydrogen tanks that were used. The tanks are shielded by a canopy of pine branches to keep them cool, so the gas does not expand and rupture the tanks.

Transporting Hydrogen. The hydrogen gas was transported to the area via railcars. The railroad did not go to the Stratobowl, so the gas had to be hauled by trucks to the launch site. Troopers from the 4th Cavalry loaded the tanks from the railcars onto the trucks.

EXPLORER II FLIGHT, NOVEMBER 1935. Machine Gun Troop, 4th Cavalry and Air Corps personnel posed for this group portrait. The 4th Cavalry provided security and logistical support as well as ground crew for the night-long inflation.

SHED FOR GAS TANKS. This is a view of the shed housing the gas tanks for the Strato balloon. There were 1,685 tanks. *Explorer II* used helium gas instead of hydrogen because it was less likely to explode. Helium has a lesser lifting ability compared to hydrogen, so the balloon had to be larger in size.

THE NIGHT BEFORE THE BIG FLIGHT. It took all night to inflate the balloon for *Explorer II*. The balloon held 3.7 million cubic feet of helium. Again, the Dow Chemical Company, of Michigan, built the gondola. It weighed 638 pounds and was nine feet in diameter. The gondola was made of Dowmetal, a magnesium alloy lighter than aluminum. The thickness of the shell was 3/16 of an inch. There were numerous instruments locate inside the gondola for the experiments that were to take place after launch. There was an 80-pound parachute added to the *Explorer II* gondola that was designed to safely allow it to descend if the balloon failed like the *Explorer* balloon did.

Inflating the Balloon. This series of photographs shows the inflation of the balloon. Three men were on each of the 36 ropes holding the upper part of the balloon and 36 floodlights illuminated the inflation process.

READY TO GO. The balloon of *Explorer II*, 192 feet in diameter, is fully inflated.

***EXPLORER II* IS LAUNCHED.** The launch occurred at 7:01 a.m. and lasted eight hours and 13 minutes.

Explorer II is in the Air, November 11, 1935. It reached an altitude of 72,395 feet, a world record at that time. *Explorer II* landed near White Lake, South Dakota.

Capt. Albert Stevens. Capt. Albert Stevens (1886–1949) was an officer in the Army Air Corps. He enlisted in the US Air Service in 1918 and served as an officer until medically discharged in 1942. Captain Stevens was awarded the Distinguished Flying Cross for both of the Stratobowl balloon flights. Capt. Orvil Anderson (1895–1965) enlisted in the US Army Signal Corps in 1917. He went to balloon observer's school and was commissioned as a second lieutenant in the US Air Service. His service continued through World War II when he was promoted to major general in February 1944. Anderson retired from the Air Force in 1950. He was also awarded the Distinguished Flying Cross for both of the Stratobowl balloon flights.

Six

World War II and Transition to VA Hospital 1944–1946

Civilian Conservation Corps. In 1933, as part of the New Deal, Congress created the Emergency Conservation Agency, later and more commonly known as the Civilian Conservation Corps (CCC). The sub-headquarters for South Dakota was established at Fort Meade and was managed by the 4th Cavalry. For the first year, enrollees were housed in the barracks and fed alongside the soldiers. This was a service detachment; jobs assigned to these enrollees were clerical and logistical. Clerks served in the CCC commissary, quartermaster's office, and hospital. Men were also assigned as truck drivers hauling supplies.

COMPANY 2758. Building a separate camp became necessary, and in July 1934, Company 2758 was established to build a camp, which became known as Camp Fechner. At the time, the 4th Cavalry remained in charge of both the company and the camp. On October 31, 1935, Company 2758 was demobilized, and most of the men were transferred to Camp Estes.

TENT CAMP. While building Camp Fechner, Company 2758 resided in tents. This photograph is dated August 1934. The mess hall, the bathhouse, and the latrine were finished in August that year, but the barracks were not completed until October.

CAMP FECHNER. Camp Fechner was located in a picturesque bowl surrounded by pine trees on the west edge of Fort Meade. Ten barracks were arranged in a semicircle with a 300-foot radius. The officers' quarters overlooked the camp from the hill above. The axis of the camp went from the officers' quarters through to the mess hall. Camp formed at T with the headquarters at the entrance to the camp and the recreation hall across camp. The road coming into the camp ran past headquarters and perpendicular to the axis. Gravel walks connected the buildings.

SCS-6. After Company 2758 was demobilized, the camp briefly served as the sub-headquarters. The camp was reopened in October 1936 as CCC Camp SCS-6 (Soil Conservation Service). The work of this company focused on soil and moisture conservation. Their activities included demonstrations in furrow and contour farming, building stock water dams, and planting trees. They worked both on private and forest land.

ROBERT FECHNER. Camp Fechner was named for Robert Fechner, a labor leader who was appointed by President Roosevelt as the director of the Civilian Conservation Corps. Although he only had an elementary school education, he became the vice president of the International Association of Machinists and a prominent American labor leader. He was considered a fair, patient, and tactful man. While he had much experience as a labor leader, he discouraged unionization among the CCCs, believing that the government was meeting the needs of the enrollees. In this photograph, an unidentified man stands in front of the camp entrance sign.

Walking around Camp. This candid photograph of men walking around camp shows the construction of the stone paths between the buildings. Four of the 10 barracks comprising the semicircle are seen in the background. The flagpole is at left, and what appears to be an information center is in the center of the photograph.

In Line at the Mess Hall. The mess hall ran perpendicular to the barracks buildings, again seen in the background with the flagpole and information center on the left side of the photograph. Initially the enrollees were between the ages of 17 and 22. Housing, food, and clothing were provided, and they received $30 a month. They were encouraged to send most of that home to their families.

Inside the Barracks. Enrollees worked a hard 40 hours a week. They had a strict routine of when to rise and when to retire for the night. But the experience provided valuable employment and training as well as enabling them to help support their families through the Depression. Enrollment periods were for six months with the option to reenroll. At first, the age limit was 17–22. However, it was later determined that it was helpful to have older men who were already skilled as leaders. The age limit was also relaxed for needy veterans.

Camp Remnants. In June 1942, President Roosevelt moved to abolish the CCC within 12 months. The United States had entered the Second World War seven months prior, and the young men working at the camps were needed in the armed forces. Six months later, President Roosevelt declared the CCC camps closed. This photograph shows the fireplace from the officers' quarters at Camp Fechner.

88TH GLIDER CORPS. Fort Meade played a part in the Normandy invasion. The 88th Glider Infantry Regiment, commanded by Col. Joseph Hinton, was part of the 1st Airborne Infantry Brigade. Brig. Gen. Leo Donovan commanded the brigade and established his headquarters at Fort Meade. Donovan's command included troops stationed at Alliance Nebraska. Pilot training and parachute jumping training took place at Alliance Airbase. Soldiers stationed at Fort Meade trained in combat readiness and infantry tactics such as forced night marches. They also trained for parachute drops and loading troops and equipment into cargo aircraft. The 88th left Fort Meade for training at Camp McCall North Carolina and went on to England for the Normandy invasion.

Stone Facing on Buildings. In the 1930s, the WPA worked at Fort Meade putting stone facades such as this one on old wooden structures. This small house was built on the site of the old post office. On the 1937 map, it is listed as NCO housing.

Custer Hall. In the early 1940s, Fort Meade made some changes to accommodate the expected influx of troops. One of these upgrades was to build Custer Hall. The building served as a banquet and dance hall, and it held a library. During the war, it served as a Red Cross center. The post radio station was also housed here.

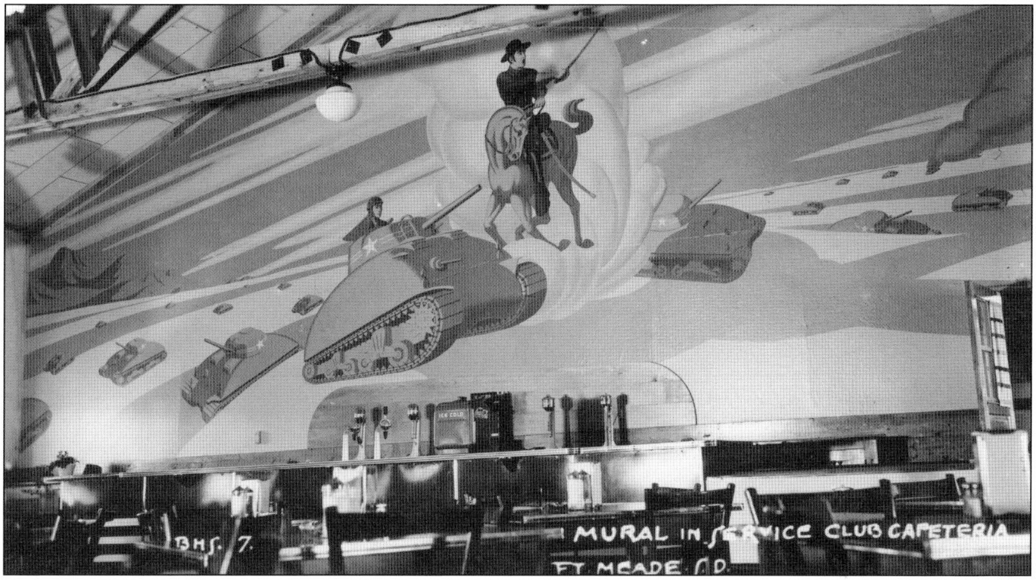

Murals. On November 1, 1942, the 620th Engineer General Service Company arrived at Fort Meade. They were a special unit filled with enlisted men who were suspected of being enemy sympathizers. Typically, they were of German or Italian origin. Companies like this were stationed far from where they could conduct subversive activities. They were not armed, but otherwise they could come and go as freely as any other soldier. They were assigned various maintenance and construction duties. It was these soldiers who painted these murals in Custer Hall.

Aerial View. This photograph gives an excellent view of the terrain surrounding Fort Meade. The fort is seen in the foreground, and the natural bowl formed by the hills to the south is easily seen here. The city of Sturgis can be seen to the west of the heavily forested area of Bear Butte Pass.

Prisoners of War (POW). The isolation of posts such as Fort Meade made them desirable places for confining POWs. An added advantage of Fort Meade was Camp Fechner. By installing fences and barbed wire, the former CCC camp was readily available for detaining German POWs. While interred at Fort Meade, the prisoners were put to work in two ways. First, they were sent to harvest sugar beets near Belle Fourche, South Dakota. Second, they were assigned construction duties around the post. There was a second POW camp near Orman Dam in Butte County, close to Belle Fourche. Visual documentation of the POWs presence in the Black Hills is sparse. One physical remnant of their time here is this piece of sidewalk marked by POW 256 in 1946 and preserved in the Old Fort Meade Museum. Another piece is the inscription from some unnamed detainee carved into the step of the current post office. (Courtesy of Lee Stroschine.)

Transition. As World War II drew to a close, changing military needs diminished the usefulness of small posts such as Fort Meade. The War Department suggested turning Fort Meade over to the Veterans Administration (VA). The VA was experiencing an increased need for hospitals, particularly for neuropsychiatric care. Sen. Francis Case petitioned them to consider Fort Meade for conversion to one of these hospitals. Early in 1944, Fort Meade was deemed suitable for this purpose. In May, President Roosevelt approved the transfer of Fort Meade to the Veterans Administration. On June 11, 1944, Congress passed an act to transfer Fort Meade to the Veterans Administration.

Conversion to a Hospital. South Dakota senator Francis Case saw to it that $300,000 was appropriated for the conversion. Skilled civilian workmen were in short supply due to the war, so to advance the project at the desired pace, in November over 100 German prisoners of war from Fort Robinson, Nebraska, were brought in to assist with the work. They were guarded by US soldiers also from Fort Robinson. Conversion completed, the hospital was dedicated on Army Day, April 6, 1945.

Hospital Fire Department. The Fort Meade Veterans Administration Hospital needed the services of a small town. Here is the Fort Meade VA Hospital Fire Department in the early 1940s. The fire station building is one of the many temporary structures erected during the 1930s and 1940s. Most of these temporary buildings have since been disassembled.

MODERNIZATION. The converted barracks were used as the hospital wards until 1967, when the VA completed a major modernization project. Behind the row of barracks, three modern hospital buildings were constructed in 1959, 1960, and 1966. These photographs show the before and after layout of Fort Meade's original buildings and the new hospital structures.

Expanded Mission. The original mission of the Veterans Administration hospital at Fort Meade was to serve veterans in need of neuropsychiatric care. However, in order to address the needs of more veterans of the Black Hills region, services were expanded to include general and surgical care. The name was changed to Fort Meade Veterans Administration Medical Center in 1973 to reflect the expanded mission.

Bibliography

Agnew, Jeremy. *Life of a Soldier on the Western Frontier.* Missoula, MT: Mountain Press Publishing, 2008.

Cleveland, Herbert B. *Fort Meade, D.T., S.D., 1878–1978: 100 years of service.* Sturgis, SD: Veterans Administration Hospital (Fort Meade), 1978.

Lee, Robert. *Fort Meade and the Black Hills.* Lincoln, NE: University of Nebraska Press, 1991.

———. *Fort Meade the Peace Keeper Post on the Dakota Frontier 1878–1944.* Sturgis, SD: Old Fort Meade Museum & Research Association, 1987.

"Man's Farthest Aloft." *National Geographic.* January 1936: 58–94

Pengra, Lilah Morton. *Corporals, Cooks and Cowboys: African Americans in the Black Hills and Surrounding Areas.* Buffalo Gap, SD: L.M. Pengra, 2005.

"Studies Planned for New Stratosphere Flight with Helium." *National Geographic.* June 1935: 794–800.

"The Society Announces New Flight into the Stratosphere." *National Geographic.* February 1935: 265–272.

"World's Largest Free Balloon to Explore Stratosphere." *National Geographic.* July 1934: 107–110